'Here's looking
with love

Andrey x

'Here's looking
with love

HOLLYWOOD
COCKTAILS

HOLLYWOOD
COCKTAILS

TOBIAS STEED
with cocktail recipes by
BEN REED

MITCHELL BEAZLEY

HOLLYWOOD COCKTAILS
by Tobias Steed and Ben Reed

First published in Great Britain in 1999 by Mitchell Beazley, an
imprint of Octopus Publishing Group Limited,
2–4 Heron Quays, London E14 4JP.

A CIP catalogue record for this book is available
from the British Library.

ISBN 1 84000 199 2

The author and publishers will be grateful for any information
that will assist them in keeping future editions up to date.
Although all reasonable care has been taken in the preparation
of this book, neither the publishers nor the author can accept
any liability for any consequences arising from the use thereof,
or the information contained therein.

Commissioning Editor: Margaret Little
Art Director: Gaye Allen
Managing Editor: Hilary Lumsden
Editor: Jamie Ambrose
Designer: Colin Goody
Picture Research: Jenny Faithful and Helen Stallion
Production Controller: Rachel Staveley

Typeset in Kabel, Shannon and Bell Centennial

Printed and bound by Toppan Printing Company in China

AUTHOR'S NOTE
It is for the reader's attention that the cocktail recipes listed may not
always correspond to those actually featured in the films in question.
And that the quotations used, although taken from the films in
question, may not always corresond to the particular scenes shown.

DEDICATION
To my very own "Gibson girl", Catherine, and to my dear friend Chris
– the glasses are chilled and the next Martini is on me.

CONTENTS

INTRODUCTION

What better place to start sampling the sheer glitz and glamour of the world of cocktails than the silver screen? Here you'll find drinks for every mood: sultry seductions, cheery celebrations and moments of reflection and melancholy; and drinks for every occasion: intimate conversations, raucous parties and glamorous galas. These elegant tipples evoke the effortless style and sophistication of the classic movies in which they play a part.

These days it's hard to find a barperson who hasn't designed a range of elaborate concoctions that include every imaginable extra – multiple spirits, fruit juices, exotic mixers – none of these come close to the original drinks of old Hollywood, when a good cocktail was only a couple of shakes away.

For our selection of cocktails, we have tried to heed a golden rule of good cocktail making: keep it simple. We have concentrated on classic cocktails that have passed the test of time. Our aim has been to gather together a discerning collection, where occasionally the inclusion of a new ingredient or substitution of a spirit can create an interesting variation or an entirely different drink. It is our hope that aspiring cocktail enthusiasts will learn the basic ingredients and steps for even just a few classic cocktails fairly quickly.

With just a little practise, you too can learn how to mix a delectable drink to arouse the appetite, raise a toast, aid the digestion or settle the stomach after a night's worth of experimentation – all the while having tremendous fun.

We have also aimed to achieve our own delicate balance of memorable films and memorable drinks. In these pages you will find a parade of screen legends spotted sipping in key scenes from their movies, from William Powell and Myrna Loy to Greta Garbo, Clark Gable, Bogart and Bacall, Bette Davis and a cast of thousands.

Hollywood is sometimes accused of being unduly influential upon us, and we freely admit to drawing on the unique style of its golden age and the debonair grace with which many of its matinée idols savoured their cocktails. We hope you enjoy making and sampling your own Hollywood cocktails as much as we have enjoyed bringing them together.

COCKTAIL ETIQUETTE

THE RIGHT SCENE

Hollywood cocktails are all about glamour. You only have to watch the movies. Whenever did you see David Niven or Gregory Peck looking less than impeccably suave and sophisticated, or stars like Lauren Bacall and Audrey Hepburn without gloves or a hat – or at the very least a feather boa?

You may make the best cocktails in the world, but if you're rustling them up in a messy kitchen with loud rock music blaring in the background you might just as well be making a cup of instant coffee. For the full effect you need to set the scene, and that means soft music (jazz maybe), softer still lighting and a sofa that isn't strewn with beer cans and old newspapers.

It's *de rigueur* to dress up for a cocktail. Maybe a white dinner jacket is a bit over the top these days, but a crisp, freshly ironed shirt will do you no harm at all. And no woman ever lost her man by pulling on a pair of sheer silk stockings, pouring herself into a figure-hugging little black dress and trailing a discreet scent of expensive French perfume. Think Audrey Hepburn. Think *Breakfast at Tiffany's...*

THE RIGHT KIT...

You may not have a cocktail cabinet but there's no reason why you can't present your cocktails with panache and flair. A black lacquer tray, a couple of different types of glass (a classic Martini glass and a Highball glass) and

a cocktail shaker and you're in business. Shakers come in many different shapes and sizes. The Boston shaker is perhaps the best – ½ stainless steel, ½ glass. The final touch is to indulge in a barspoon – teaspoon size, with a "helter-skelter" stem to allow smooth and gentle pouring.

...AND INGREDIENTS

If you're going to make knockout Hollywood-style cocktails it's always best to use top-quality ingredients, particularly in drinks such as Margaritas or Daiquiris, where the fine balance of the drink can be affected if you don't use fresh lime juice.

If you're going to have bottles on show to create the right sophisticated impression, it's far more stylish to use brands your guests will recognise, rather than cut-price bargains you've picked up at a discount store. The basic necessities are a bottle of gin – try Bombay Sapphire or Tanqueray – a bottle of vodka – Russian, of course – and a bottle of vermouth. And don't forget the Angostura bitters. Exotic ingredients like orgeat syrup (almond-flavoured syrup) can be found in specialist food and drink shops.

Some cocktail aficionados turn up their noses at an inappropriate garnish, and, when it comes to the classics, it's crucial to get it right. Never put a celery stick in a Vodka Martini or, for that matter, an olive in a Bloody Mary. With newer cocktails you can be more experimental as long as the garnish complements the taste of the drink. But at the end of the day cocktails are supposed to be fun, so if you want to bung a sparkler in your drink – fine. Just watch your eyebrows!

THE RIGHT TECHNIQUE

Half the fun of making Hollywood cocktails is to do it in front of your guests, but to make a good impression you'll have just one take. So it's best to have one or two cocktails you know how to do really well – practise beforehand so that it looks as if you've been pouring them all your life.

If you're following our recipes use the same measures to start with. Our single shot is 25ml and a double is 50ml. A dash is... well, a dash, and a large dash about twice that (barpersons never measure). But do alter the recipe if the cocktail is too sweet or too strong for your personal taste.

Most cocktails in Britain are served far too warm, so if you want to make them the Hollywood way make sure you have plenty of ice to hand (made with mineral rather than tap water for a cleaner taste). You can also frost your glasses beforehand by leaving them in the fridge for an hour.

Shaken, stirred or straight up? Some people swear that shaking is preferable to stirring. With others it's just the reverse. Choose the method most comfortable for you. The point is to mix the drink and get it cold – either way you don't want to overdo it. A drink that has been shaken too long will lose its concentration and end up resembling a slush puppie – you should just give it a quick shake and leave it at that. Even if you prefer your drink stirred you shouldn't do it too energetically or you'll break up the ice. And if your guest asks for his or her Martini "straight up" you should oblige. After all it's the role of the cocktail maker to put his or her guests at ease.

AFTER OFFICE HOURS

THE COCKTAIL HOUR

In Hollywood films the cocktail hour was used as a time of transformation, giving filmmakers the chance to pause from the action and develop their narratives. It was also, of course, a time for reflection and refreshment – as eloquently explained by composer Cole Porter who compared "gin and vermouth" to the "fountain of youth".

For many, the cocktail hour signalled the first drink of the day. For others, like WC Fields – "I never drink anything stronger than gin before breakfast" – time was simply a relative matter...

Yet, whenever and wherever drinks are served, the most popular cocktail of all is still the Martini, as classically Hollywood as "lights, camera, action!"

The debate over the origins of the Martini will rage as long as there are bars. While most often associated with vermouth-producer Martini & Rossi, many claim that Martini di Arma di Taggia, bartender at New York's Knickerbocker Hotel, mixed the first "dry" Martini in the late 19th century. What constitutes it remains hotly contested. Some bartenders prefer a dash of vermouth, others just whisper the name over the glass.

DRY MARTINI

AFTER OFFICE HOURS (1935)

The three-Martini lunch had not yet become compulsory for the newspaper set when Clark Gable teamed up with Constance Bennett in *After Office Hours*, but the film may well have helped link the drink with the industry. In this MGM comedy, Gable – otherwise known as the "King of Hollywood" – plays the role of Jim Branch, a newspaper editor who becomes involved in trying to solve a murder mystery. Here, Branch and the paper's socialite reporter Sharon Norwood (Bennett) wet their lips with an after-hours Martini while discussing their next moves.

50 ML GIN

DRY VERMOUTH

1 GREEN OLIVE OR LEMON ZEST

Add a couple of drops of vermouth into a mixing glass filled with ice; stir gently and strain out excess liquid. Add more ice, the gin and stir again. Wait until the mixing glass has frosted, then strain into a chilled Martini glass. Garnish with either a strip of lemon zest or a green olive. This drink can also be served over ice in a rocks glass.

SHARON NORWOOD *"Why did you lie to me?"*

JIM BRANCH *"If you were looking at what I'm looking at, you'd know why I lied to you."*

ALL ABOUT EVE (1950)

Twelve Oscar nominations and six awards, including Best Picture, Best Director and Best Screenplay for a savvy script that removes the make-up and reveals the backstage back-stabbing of Broadway. Bette Davis (below) plays Margo Channing, a great Broadway actress who takes a star-struck Eve Harrington (Anne Baxter) under her wing. Set in the tumultuous world of the New York theatre, *All About Eve* follows Eve's manipulations into the diva's life and career. "Fasten your seat-belts: it is going to be a bumpy night" – Margo warns early on of a turbulent journey to come, but audiences stayed riveted to their seats, awaiting the final outcome of *All About Eve*.

The Gibson is a variation of a Martini: just replace the olive with a pearl onion. There seems to be no doubt that the original imbiber was named Gibson. The leading contender is Charles Dana Gibson, creator of the "Gibson Girl" – America's first glamour girl – based on his wife Irene. But an array of Gibsons – from an ambassadorial representative to Chicago twin sisters – have also entered the frame.

GIBSON

50 ML GIN (OR VODKA)

DRY VERMOUTH (NOILLY PRAT)

1 PEARL COCKTAIL ONION

Fill a mixing glass with ice and pour in a few drops of dry vermouth. Stir for 15 seconds, or until vermouth has coated the ice, then strain out the liquid. Top up mixing glass with ice, add gin and stir until glass is frosted and the mixture is well chilled. Pour into a chilled Martini glass, or over ice into a rocks glass. Garnish with a pearl cocktail onion.

MARGO *"I admit I may have seen better days, but I'm still not to be had for the price of a cocktail like a salted peanut."*

How dry is dry? Bartenders the world over have created and poured their own versions of the Martini in an endless quest for the ultimate "dry" Martini. Usually dryness is dictated by the ratio of gin to vermouth: the more gin, the drier the result. In this recipe, vodka replaces gin to make a Vodka Martini, or "Vodkatini" as it is also known. It first appeared as an alternative in 1951, but achieved fame courtesy of James Bond.

VODKA MARTINI

MY MAN GODFREY (1957)

In this remake of the classic Universal comedy, illegal immigrant "Godfrey" (David Niven, left) poses as a roguish sailor and meets society girl Irene Bullock (June Allyson) during a scavenger hunt. He subsequently becomes butler to her upper-class family, which has more than its fair share of spoiled debutantes. In his new position, Godfrey spends much of his time fetching trays of Martinis – most of which are rarely drunk due to the daughters' eternal bickering. Thus it is that Godfrey, who in reality is an Austrian count, helps himself to the odd trayful to escape the Bullocks' constant histrionics.

50 ML VODKA

DRY VERMOUTH

1 GREEN OLIVE OR LEMON ZEST

Add a couple of drops of vermouth into a mixing glass filled with ice; stir gently and strain out excess liquid. Add more ice, the vodka and stir again. Wait until the mixing glass has frosted, then strain into a chilled Martini glass. Garnish with either a strip of lemon zest or a green olive. This drink can also be served over ice in a rocks glass.

MAN AT BAR *"Get a load of the dizzy dame with the monkey."*

MR BULLOCK *"I've been getting a load of her for 30 years. That's my wife."*

50 ML GIN

LARGE DASH DRY VERMOUTH

SMALL DASH SWEET VERMOUTH

*Add the gin and both vermouths
to a mixing glass filled with ice.
Once well mixed, strain into a
frosted Martini glass.*

KNICKERBOCKER

Mixing Martinis with marriage and – in the case of *The Thin Man* – a little murder, is certain to stir up trouble. This cocktail, unlike its cousin the Martini, uses a measurable amount of gin and dry vermouth, with a dash of sweet vermouth to balance. Its origins are uncertain, but its name suggests that they might have been at the Knickerbocker Hotel in New York.

THE THIN MAN (1934)

Based on the 1932 detective novel by Dashiell Hammett, Nick and Nora (William Powell and Myrna Loy, above) charmed critics and cinema-goers with their comedy, crime-fighting and canine companion Asta. The constant drinking of this jovial, bantering couple never hampered their investigative skills – quite the opposite, in fact. "Can't you say anything about the case?" a detective asks. "Yes," Nick grumbles. "It's putting me way behind in my drinking." The duo's great success led to four Oscar nominations and five additional "Thin Man" films.

NICK TO BARMAN *"A Manhattan you shake to foxtrot time. A Bronx to er, two-step time. A Dry Martini you always shake to waltz time."*

The "It" in question refers to sweet red vermouth. Purists would be horrified to see Vincent Price mixing such a drink, but the red vermouth and a squeeze of orange juice provided a sweeter cocktail that proved particularly popular with the ladies. As to the name, all we know for certain is that, early in the 20th century, the Martini was frequently referred to by Europeans as a "Gin and It".

······· GIN AND IT

30 ML GIN

30 ML SWEET RED VERMOUTH

Stir the gin and vermouth together over ice in a mixing glass. When mixed well, strain into a frosted Martini glass to serve.

LAURA (1944)

A fine detective thriller, *Laura* is a beautifully constructed piece of filmmaking with a great development of suspense. A woman's body is found in a New York apartment, brutally murdered and unrecognisable. Police assume she's the owner, Laura Hunt, played by Gene Tierney. Detective McPherson (Dana Andrews) becomes fascinated by Laura's life. When the real Laura reappears after a trip to the country, McPherson's interest turns to love. There's just one problem, however: Laura is now a suspect in the murder case. Fine performances from Clifton Webb and Vincent Price (right) as suspects Waldo Lydecker and Shelby Carpenter bring the film to a compelling but macabre conclusion.

SHELBY CARPENTER *"I can afford a blemish on my character, but not on my clothes."*

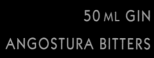

50 ML GIN

ANGOSTURA BITTERS

*Add a few drops of Angostura
bitters to a Martini glass, roll
around, then shake out. Add ice
and gin and serve. (Can be served
without ice, if you prefer.)*

PINK GIN

For centuries, gin has been a traditional part of the British armed forces' medicine chest. In fact, the Gin and Tonic arose from an attempt to mask the bitter flavour of the anti-malarial quinine that was issued to troops in Africa and India. In a similar fashion, the Pink Gin is said to have been invented by British sailors, who mixed their gin rations with Angostura bitters, a medicinal herb extract that was prescribed for digestive distress.

DARK VICTORY (1939)

Unfortunately, 1939 was the year *Gone with the Wind* ran away with the Oscars; otherwise, Bette Davis (above, left) might well have captured her third with her portrayal of Judith Traherne, a dizzy heiress stricken with a brain tumour. Her poignant performance quashed Jack Warner's "Who wants to see a dame go blind?" cynicism by pulling in a huge audience who appreciated the pathos. The film also featured Ronald Reagan, Humphrey Bogart, George Brent (above) as Davis' love interest, and Geraldine Fitzgerald (above, centre) in her American debut.

JUDITH TRAHERNE *"Confidentially, honey, this is more than a hangover."*

The imperial stamp of approval given by William of Orange (1689–1702) and his queen, Mary, popularised that juniper-flavoured spirit, gin. Developed for medicinal purposes in 1650, it is likely that gin, a contraction of the Dutch *genever*, was actually made before then. The term "Dutch Courage" was coined by the English soldiers who would drink a bracer with their Dutch comrades before battle.

IMPERIAL

30 ML GIN

30 ML DRY VERMOUTH

DASH OF ANGOSTURA BITTERS

DASH OF MARASCHINO JUICE

1 GREEN OLIVE

Stir all ingredients over ice in a mixing glass. When well mixed together, strain into a frosted Martini glass and garnish with a cocktail olive.

JEFF HOLLAND *"Here's to us!"*

LINDA BRONSON *"The three of us!"*

SKY AMES *"My best pal, my best gal!"*

REMEMBER? (1939)

Remember? was only Greer Garson's second movie, and her first in a major starring role, alongside Robert Taylor and Lew Ayres. In this triangular comedy Ayres plays Sky Ames (below, right), a chemist in a patent medicine company who is engaged to Linda Bronson (Garson, below). When Sky introduces his fiancée to Jeff Holland (Taylor, below, left), they fall in love, have a difficult marriage and finally divorce. Meanwhile, one of Sky's colleagues invents a drug that induces amnesia, he uses that on the couple to make them forget the past in the hope of a new outcome. It works like a charm: Jeff and Linda forget their liaison – only to re-enact it by falling in love all over again!

DRY CHAMPAGNE

25 ML BRANDY

1 WHITE SUGAR CUBE

ANGOSTURA BITTERS

*Douse the sugar cube in
Angostura bitters and place into a
Champagne flute. Add the brandy,
then gently top up with Champagne.*

CHAMPAGNE COCKTAIL

Believed to have originated in the southern states of America, the Champagne
Cocktail has been an essential prop and elegant aid to seduction for many leading lights
of the silver screen. Like the Martini, dryness is paramount, and *brut* Champagne is
a must. Never out of style, it remains a classic to this day – just like *Casablanca* itself.

CASABLANCA (1942)

A veritable "cocktail" of refugees passed through the Café Americain in *Casablanca*. And a multitude of cocktails passed through their lips, always served by Carl, the head waiter (SZ Sakall), and usually accompanied by piano music from the faithful Sam (Dooley Wilson, above, left). Rick Blaine, played by

Humphrey Bogart (above), uttered some of the most memorable lines in screen history. His immortal "We'll always have Paris" recalls the happier, less complicated days of his existence as shown above, when he shares a glass of Champagne with Ilsa Lund, played by Ingrid Bergman, and Sam at La Belle Aurore in Paris.

A popular drink for receptions and soirées, as well as the cocktail hour, the Kir Royale blends *crème de cassis*, a blackcurrant liqueur, with Champagne for a velvety taste sensation. Named after Canon Felix Kir, the original Kir was invented in France and made with still, dry white wine. To get the "Royale" treatment, however, *brut* (dry) Champagne is essential.

KIR ROYALE

THE PHILADELPHIA STORY (1940)

If you thought intrusive paparazzi were only a present-day phenomenon, then you've never seen *The Philadelphia Story*, based on the 1939 play by Philip Barry. Katharine Hepburn (left) plays Tracy Lord, a young, beautiful, head-strong and divorced East Coast socialite preparing to marry for the second time. Macauley Connor (James Stewart, left) and Elizabeth Imbrie (Ruth Hussey) have been assigned by a society magazine to cover the events leading up to, and after, the wedding. Add Cary Grant as Tracy's suave ex-husband CK Dexter Haven, and a classic, sophisticated comedy emerges. Witty dialogue flows as fast and easily as Champagne. In 1956, the film was remade as the musical *High Society* – but, sadly, without the same cachet.

MACAULEY CONNOR TO TRACY LORD

"Whisky's a slap on the back, and Champagne is a heavy mist before my eyes."

10 ML CREME DE CASSIS
DRY CHAMPAGNE

Pour the crème de cassis *into a Champagne flute, then fill slowly with chilled dry Champagne.*

For the original Kir, substitute chilled still dry white wine for the Champagne.

EVERY DAY'S A HOLIDAY (1937)

Flamboyant, farcical and flippant, Mae West is Peaches O'Day (above), a con artist who sells the Brooklyn Bridge, gets chased out of town by the New York Police Department, and masquerades as Mademoiselle Fifi, a French revue singer. Set in the Big Apple of the 1890s, *Every Day's a Holiday* features some fine work from Charles Butterworth, who, as Larmadou Graves (above, far left), quips: "You ought to get out of those clothes and into a Dry Martini". The supporting cast includes Walter Catlett as Nifty Bailey (above, second from left) and Charles Winninger as Van Reighle Van Pelter Van Doon (far right). There is also a cameo by the legendary Louis Armstrong. West, who claimed to have invented censorship, gives one of her finer performances, and her last for Paramount.

FRESH PEACH JUICE
DRY CHAMPAGNE

Make sure that your ingredients are well chilled for this cocktail. Half fill a Champagne flute with peach juice, top up with the Champagne and stir. Serve chilled.

BELLINI

A Bellini is just the drink for Peaches O'Day. Inspired by the work of the 15th-century Italian painter Giovanni Bellini – on account of the glowing pinks in his paintings – this delicious pairing of Champagne and peach juice was created by Giuseppi Cipriani at Harry's Bar in Venice during the early 1940s.

LARMADOU GRAVES *"May I sit on your right hand?"*

PEACHES O'DAY *"You better sit in the chair."*

BACARDI COCKTAIL

Any bartender may find himself permanently behind bars if he doesn't use Bacardi rum here. Founded in 1862 by Don Facundo Bacardi in Santiago de Cuba, Bacardi is the best-selling brand of rum in the world, and in 1936, the company won a court action in New York protecting the use of its brand name in this cocktail.

50 ML BACARDI WHITE RUM
1 TEASPOON GRENADINE
SMALL DASH OF FRESH LIME
OR LEMON JUICE

Pour the ingredients into a cocktail shaker. Shake sharply and strain into a frosted Martini glass.

CAMPARI COCKTAIL

Any bartender may find himself permanently behind bars if he doesn't use Bacardi rum here. Founded in 1862 by Don Facundo Bacardi in Santiago de Cuba, Bacardi is the best-selling brand of rum in the world, and in 1936, the company won a court action in New York protecting the use of its brand name in this cocktail.

Pour the ingredients into a cocktail shaker filled with ice and shake sharply. Strain into a frosted Martini glass.

40 ML VODKA
50 ML CAMPARI
DASH OF ANGOSTURA BITTERS

40 ML DUBONNET

20 ML GIN

ORANGE ZEST

Pour both ingredients into a mixing glass filled with ice. Stir and strain into a frosted Martini glass. Garnish with a strip of orange zest.

DUBONNET COCKTAIL

Dubonnet originally hailed from France and is a vermouth flavoured with quinine and bitter barks. It is much sweeter than Campari, or even red vermouth, and is now produced in both red and white versions. This cocktail makes a classic *apéritif*, and this version uses the original aromatic red Dubonnet.

60 ML DRY OR SWEET VERMOUTH

DASH OF ANGOSTURA BITTERS

Stir ingredients well in a mixing glass filled with ice, then strain into a frosted Martini glass.

VERMOUTH COCKTAIL

Originally created as a medicinal tonic, vermouth is the generic name for white wine infused with herbs, brandy, sugar and water. Wormwood (from the German *Wermut*) is an essential ingredient and lends the beverage its name, but all vermouth manufacturers guard the secret of their exact blends very closely. Today's main brands are Martini & Rossi, Cinzano, Noilly Prat and Punt e Mes.

DINNER AT EIGHT

APERITIFS & DIGESTIFS

Seminal though it is, the Martini is not the be-all and end-all of cocktails. For many, real pleasure is derived from the diversity of choice. Short, long, neat or over ice, there are as many types of cocktails as there are films.

Before dining, for example, comes the apéritif, which, like a cinematic preview, arouses interest in the main event. After the meal, it's time for the digestif – the credits, if you will, which round off the whole occasion.

Today, we tend to drink what we like when we like, but as film buffs know, the magic of the movies lies in the total experience. To truly savour a cocktail, then, choose the right time and place.

50ML RYE WHISKEY

25ML SWEET VERMOUTH

ORANGE BITTERS

ORANGE ZEST

MARASCHINO CHERRY

Pour the whiskey, the vermouth and the bitters into an ice-filled mixing glass. Stir until the mixture is chilled and blended, then strain into a frosted Martini glass. Garnish with a Maraschino cherry and a strip of orange zest.

MANHATTAN

After the Martini, the Manhattan became the most popular pre-dinner drink in the United States; it also formed the foundation of many other cocktails. Starring whiskey in the lead role rather than gin, this cocktail was named after New York's Manhattan Club. Some say it was invented at the request of Lady Randolph Churchill, mother of Winston.

MURDER AT THE VANITIES (1934)

Like Ziegfeld's Follies, Earl Carroll's Vanities staged a lavish Broadway revue during the 1920s. *Murder at the Vanities* is a comical musical murder mystery, written by Earl Carroll himself together with mystery writer Rufus King. During character Rita Ross' (Gertrude Michael) performance of a song called "Sweet Marijuana", a woman's body is found high in the rafters. Suspicion falls upon all backstage and it is left to Detective Bill Murdock (Victor McLaglen) to sort through the ensuing carnage.

Duke Ellington and his orchestra provide the musical entertainment, and this film is the source of that tippler's classic "Cocktails for Two".

BILL MURDOCK *"Her next change will be in a wooden kimono. She's dead."*

The simplest variation on the Manhattan is the Rob Roy, which employs Scotch whisky instead of Canadian Club, bourbon or rye. Named after the Scottish hero Rob Roy, this drink can be enjoyed all year round, but it makes an especially appropriate libation for such tartan celebrations as Burns' Night (January 25th) or St Andrew's Day (November 30th).

ROB ROY

50 ML SCOTCH WHISKY

40 ML SWEET VERMOUTH

4 DROPS ANGOSTURA BITTERS

ORANGE ZEST

MARASCHINO CHERRY

Pour the whisky, vermouth and bitters into an ice-filled mixing glass. Stir until the mixture is chilled and blended, then strain into a frosted Martini glass. Garnish with a Maraschino cherry and a strip of orange zest.

ANGELS OVER BROADWAY (1940)

Charles Engel (played by John Qualen) stumbles into the Aladdin Café off Broadway to drink his life away after being caught in the act of embezzling. Enter gentlemanly crook Bill O'Brien (Douglas Fairbanks Jr, right), who mistakes Engel for a millionaire and plans a little embezzling of his own, cutting a dashing figure in spite of his dastardly ways. Meanwhile, chorus girl Nina Barona (Rita Hayworth, right) sees Engel as a chance to further her career. Thomas Mitchell plays Gene Gibbons, an alcoholic, over-the-hill playwright who supplies all the film's best lines. It is he who discovers Engel's suicide note and, with O'Brien and Barona, hatches a scheme to save the man's life. The action is aided by a well-stocked bar.

BILL O'BRIEN *"You can find anything you want in New York if you know where to look for it. Romance, adventure... in New York, it's with a world-class cast."*

From Gaelic *uisge beatha*, the word whisky literally means "water of life". There are many forms of this life-giving spirit, so stock your bar with several Scotch and Canadian types, but be sure to include American and Irish versions as well. Like any good film, the quality of whisky – with or without the "e" – depends upon a variety of elements. Single malts have the stage presence to stand alone, whereas blends require a whole cast of characters.

··· SCOTCH MIST

THE BIG SLEEP (1946)

The Big Sleep was the first film to star Humphrey Bogart and Lauren Bacall (as Philip Marlowe and Vivian Sternwood, left) following their marriage. Based on the Raymond Chandler's novel of the same name, the screenplay was written by fellow novelist William Faulkner. Howard Hawks' inventive direction creates a masterful thriller, which revolves around the two spoiled daughters of a retired general who have drunk, danced and gambled their way into the hands of unscrupulous blackmailers. Philip Marlowe is hired to sort it all out, and in the process finds himself knee-deep in murder and mayhem. "You know what he'll do when he comes back?" he tells Vivian. "Beat my teeth out, and then kick me in the stomach for mumbling."

50 ML SCOTCH WHISKY

ICE

LEMON ZEST

Pour the whisky into a cocktail shaker filled with ice. Shake sharply and strain into a small wine glass filled with crushed ice. Garnish with a strip of lemon zest.

PHILIP MARLOWE *"She tried to sit in my lap while I was standing up."*

40 ML SCOTCH WHISKY

40 ML STONE'S GREEN

GINGER WINE

Pour the whisky and ginger
wine over ice into a rocks glass.
Stir and serve.

WHISKY MAC

"Gif me a visky, ginger ale on the side, and don't be stingy, baby."
Just like that Greta Garbo ordered one of the first-ever drinks in talking pictures.
With a little inventiveness, what was potentially a Highball can be made
into a Whisky Mac by replacing the ginger ale with ginger wine.

ANNA CHRISTIE (1930)

In her first talking picture silent movie goddess Greta Garbo wowed cinema-goers with her accent, winning an Oscar nomination for Best Actress into the bargain. The film is based on the play by Eugene O'Neill and is a remake of the 1923 silent version. In it, Garbo plays Anna Christie (above), a girl with a secret past who falls in love with an Irish sailor named Matt Burke. Saved from the seas by Anna and her father, Chris Christopherson (George F Marion), Matt is played brilliantly by Charles Bickford – a sailor in real life before he joined the stage. The love affair is a source of friction between Matt and Anna's father, and can only be overcome once Anna reveals her secret.

Garbo talks!

After trying the Scotch Mist and the Whisky Mac, you might find you'd like something with a little more substance. A few Rusty Nails, however, and you'll need more than a tetanus injection to help you recover (see Corpse Reviver, p113). This cocktail is a post-Second World War invention. The addition of the sweet, dark-brown Drambuie softens the kick of the Scotch, and it also gives the drink a darker overtone that reflects its name.

RUSTY NAIL

50 ML SCOTCH WHISKY

25 ML DRAMBUIE

Pour the whisky and Drambuie into a mixing glass filled with ice. Stir well, then pour into a rocks glass to serve.

DON BIRMAN *"Most men lead lives of quiet desperation. I can't take quiet desperation."*

THE LOST WEEKEND (1945)

As poignant as it was ground-breaking when first released, *The Lost Weekend* recounts the story of alcoholic writer Don Birman on a bender, played disturbingly well by Ray Milland (below). Hollywood had never seen a film quite like this; if the preview audiences had had their way, neither would we. Billy Wilder's direction captures the degradation a drunk will endure to avoid sobriety. The cast included Jane Wyman as Helen St James (below), Phillip Terry as Don's brother, Nick, and Howard da Silva as the bartender. Proving its critics wrong and vindicating Paramount's decision to run it, the film won Oscars for Best Picture, Director, Actor and Screenplay.

PAL JOEY (1957)

A delightful film, *Pal Joey* is the cinematic version of a 1950 Broadway hit. Frank Sinatra gives a convincing performance as Joey Evans (above), an arrogant singer in San Francisco. As a *compère* in a seedy nightclub, he persuades hostess Vera Simpson (Rita Hayworth, above) to reveal her past career as a striptease artist, convincing her to perform for him. They become lovers; she buys Joey a nightclub of his own. When Linda English (Kim Novak) joins the payroll, however, Joey falls for her, but he and Vera ultimately get back together. The Rodgers and Hart score is accentuated by a fine rendition of "The Lady is a Tramp" – by Ol' Blue Eyes himself, of course.

JOEY EVANS *"Why don't you get out of something uncomfortable and I'll give you a small audition?"*

50 ML SCOTCH WHISKY

LARGE DASH OF BOILING WATER

1 TEASPOON POWDERED SUGAR

LEMON ZEST

- *Be careful with this one! Pour the Scotch whisky into one of two large tankards and pour the boiling water into the other. Light the whisky and pour it into the other mug, then in a continuous back-and-forth motion – the aim is to have a constant flame flowing between the two. Pass the mixture between the mugs four or five times, then pour into a rocks glass, sweeten with sugar, and garnish with a strip of lemon zest.*

BLUE BLAZER

Ol' Blue Eyes could light a flame in the heart of almost any dame, but could he make a Blue Blazer? This is not a drink for the inexperienced, and it was invented by Professor Jerry Thomas, creator of many famous cocktails, in the late 19th century. A woodcut in the *Savoy Cocktail Book* (published in 1930) shows him mixing a Blazer at New York's Metropolitan Hotel.

What's in a drink? The art of making cocktails is exactly that – an art. Should you ever feel uncertain about what a bartender is putting into your drink – a fate that unfortunately befalls Frank Bigelow in *DOA* – then stick to the simpler orders. The Highball is as simple as it gets; it's also thirst-quenching and a cinch to make. Just take a spirit, pair it with a mixer – Gin and Tonic, Scotch and soda – and enjoy!

BOURBON HIGHBALL

DOA (DEAD ON ARRIVAL) (1949)

While visiting one of Los Angeles' less reputable nightspots, Frank Bigelow (played by Edmond O'Brien, far left) is slipped something more toxic than alcohol in his cocktail. A visit to the doctor reveals deadly consequences, and the diagnosis spells doom. "Of course," says Dr MacDonald, "I'll have to notify the police. This is a case of homicide." "Homicide?" Bigelow replies. The doctor is adamant: "I don't think you fully understand, Bigelow. You've been murdered." With three days to live, Bigelow scours San Francisco and Los Angeles trying to find his murderer. This film's ingenious plot offers a leading role that any actor would die for.

50 ML BOURBON

GINGER ALE

TWIST OF LEMON

Pour the bourbon into a Highball glass filled with ice, top up with ginger ale and garnish with a twist of lemon.

WOMAN IN BAR *"Give that man a drink before he dies of thirst."*

50 ML BOURBON

1 WHITE SUGAR CUBE

ORANGE BITTERS

ORANGE ZEST

Place the sugar cube into a rocks glass and add the bourbon. Muddle the sugar and bourbon together with a barspoon. Add ice throughout the process, stirring continuously until the sugar has dissolved. Add a dash of orange bitters and serve with a strip of orange zest.

·····OLD FASHIONED

There was nothing old-fashioned about the 1940s film *Now, Voyager*, with its analytical journey into the psyche of Charlotte Vale. Invented in 1900 by a certain Colonel Pepper of Kentucky, the Old Fashioned possesses an equally complex personality – a traditional kick of bourbon coupled with the fruity flavour of orange.

NOW, VOYAGER (1942)

Based on the bestselling book by Olive Higgins Prouty, *Now, Voyager* stars Bette Davis as Charlotte Vale (above), a bitterly unhappy spinster suffering the oppressive nature of an overbearing mother (Davis' own daughter would charge her of this in later life). The psychiatric intervention of Dr Jaquith (played by Claude Rains) brings about a remarkable transformation, releasing Vale from her dowdy disposition and revealing a glamorous, modern woman. Love soon arrives in the form of Jerry Durrance (Paul Henreid, above). As he is already married, however, a platonic relationship is all either can hope for. Old-fashioned indeed.

CHARLOTTE VALE *"Oh Jerry, don't let's ask for the moon. We have the stars."*

The Sazerac is a product of the bayou culture of New Orleans, Louisiana, and its development has involved several infidelities. Originally created in the mid-19th century using Cognac and absinthe, today's recipe, in true Southern style, calls for bourbon as the primary spirit. As for the absinthe – well, you'll just have to make do with Pernod.

SAZERAC

- 50 ML BOURBON (OR RYE WHISKEY)
- SMALL DASH OF PERNOD
- PEYCHAUD BITTERS
- 1 WHITE SUGAR CUBE
- SODA
- TWIST OF LEMON

Fill a rocks glass with ice, then add the dash of Pernod; swill the Pernod and ice around the glass, then discard. Add the Peychaud-soaked sugar cube to the glass, and muddle with a splash of soda. When the sugar is dissolved, fill the glass with ice and add the bourbon. Garnish with a twist of lemon.

JACK WHEELER *"If it were not for the fact that the main occupation of American women is alimony, Americans would cheat the most."*

BELOVED INFIDEL (1959)

When writers are depicted in Hollywood movies, you can bet they'll be accompanied by alcohol – served on the rocks. *Beloved Infidel* follows the last years of real-life novelist F Scott Fitzgerald (played by Gregory Peck), when he worked in Hollywood to support his asylum-bound wife and began a relationship with British-born gossip columnist Sheilah Graham (Deborah Kerr), seen below with newspaper editor Jack Wheeler (Philip Ober). Fitzgerald had other problems than drink, however, including difficulties with writing for the silver screen. As one studio executive put it, "You write beautiful prose, Scott, but we can't photograph adjectives."

"Have you ever tried dunking a potato chip in Champagne?" Marilyn Monroe asks Tom Ewell in *The Seven Year Itch*. He hasn't, but admits to his secretary: "I'm perfectly capable of fixing my own breakfast. As a matter of fact, I had two peanut butter sandwiches and two Whiskey Sours." The first Sours were made in the mid-19th century, usually with brandy. The name comes from the bite of half a lemon – obvious after the first sip!

WHISKEY SOUR

THE SEVEN YEAR ITCH (1955)

A far cry from his *film noir*, *The Lost Weekend*, Billy Wilder tackles the lighter end of Hollywood in *The Seven Year Itch*. Richard Sherman (played by Tom Ewell, left) is a married publishing executive who suffers from an unremarkable domestic life and a hyperactive imagination. When a knock-out blonde drops into his life in the form of Marilyn Monroe (left, known only as "The Girl"), general mayhem of the Walter Mitty kind ensues. During one of his flights of fancy, Ewell re-enacts a parody of the love-on-the-beach scene in *From Here To Eternity*. Between them, Ewell and Monroe manage to reinvent quite a few cocktails – among other things, that is.

50 ML BOURBON (OR RYE WHISKEY)

40 ML FRESH LEMON JUICE

1 EGG WHITE

SUGAR SYRUP

ANGOSTURA BITTERS

STEMMED CHERRY

- *Add fresh lemon juice to a large dash of egg white, then mix this with the bourbon, a small measure of sugar syrup and two dashes of Angostura bitters. Shake vigorously with ice in a cocktail shaker, then pour straight into a rocks glass. Garnish with a stemmed cherry.*

RICHARD SHERMAN *"There's gin and vermouth. That's a Martini."*

THE GIRL (MM) *"Oh, that sounds cool! I think I'll have a glass of that – a big tall one!"*

OUR MODERN MAIDENS (1929)

Joan Crawford's last silent film was right on target when she instructed her female friends to "Hold fire 'til you see the whites of their eyes – then aim for the heart!" A thoroughly modern film, the lissom ladies of the Roaring Twenties took no prisoners. Crawford plays Billie Brown, an heiress to a small fortune, who is engaged to Gil (Douglas Fairbanks Jr – whom she married in real life the same year). Enter young diplomat, Glen Abbott – played by the splendidly named silent movie star Rod la Rocque – and Billie immediately decides to forget her toyboys. As the film's publicity put it: "She had all the boys she could use – but then she met a man."

Lunch is poured!

40 ML BRANDY

20 ML COINTREAU

20 ML FRESH LEMON JUICE

*Pour the ingredients
into a cocktail
shaker filled with ice.
Shake sharply and strain
into a Martini glass with
a sugared rim.*

SIDECAR

If sours of any sort are your game, then the Sidecar is the perfect drink for you.
As to its origins: Harry MacElhone, of the original Harry's New York Bar at "Sank
Roe Doe Noo" (5 rue Daunou), Paris, is credited with its invention in 1931. Yet,
a recipe for a Sidecar also appears in Harry Craddock's *Savoy Cocktail Book* (1930).
The first Harry used equal amounts of Cointreau, Cognac and lemon juice; Harry
Craddock doubled the brandy.

At first glance, the White Lady seems to be a Sidecar made with gin (instead of brandy) and an egg white – and indeed it is. Yet whereas the problem of who created the Sidecar remains unsolved, it is certain that the White Lady was created by Harry MacElhone in 1919, at Ciro's Club in London. Originally made with *crème de menthe*, in 1929, in Paris, Harry substituted gin. Perhaps the Sidecar, after all, is the descendant of the White Lady.

······ WHITE LADY

IT HAPPENED ONE NIGHT (1934)

It Happened One Night was a huge success, winning the top five Academy Awards of Best Picture, Director, Actor, Actress and Best Adaptation. Claudette Colbert plays Ellie Andrews (left), an heiress whose choice in marriage is not favoured by her father, Alexander Andrews (Walter Connolly). Connolly places her under guard aboard his yacht in Miami, but his daughter jumps ship, embarking on a cross-country bus trip to find her fiancé. Along the way she meets Peter Warne (Clark Gable), a reporter who hitches along, sensing a story. While travelling together, they fall in love, despite Warne's protests that Ellie's "just a headline to me". This delightful film established Frank Capra as a director and launched Gable and Colbert to stardom.

50 ML GIN
FRESH LEMON JUICE
TRIPLE SEC
EGG WHITE

Mix together the gin, a large dash of lemon juice, a dash of Triple Sec, and the egg white. Shake in a cocktail shaker and strain into a frosted Martini glass.

To make a Pink Lady add a dash of grenadine and an extra splash of gin.

ELLIE ANDREWS *"Well, here's to the merry-go-round."*

If you know how to make a Sour, then making a Gin Fizz is just a short splash of soda away. A Ramos Gin Fizz, however, uses extra ingredients, including an egg white. Another classic that hails from New Orleans, the Ramos Gin Fizz is sometimes called a New Orleans Fizz. It is the creation (circa 1890) of the Ramos brothers of New Orleans, who kept the recipe a secret until Prohibition (1920–33).

······ RAMOS GIN FIZZ

50 ML GIN

40 ML LEMON JUICE

DASH OF SUGAR SYRUP

DASH OF FRESH SINGLE CREAM

DASH OF EGG WHITE

3 DASHES ORANGE FLOWER WATER

SODA (OPTIONAL)

Shake all of the ingredients, except the soda, in a cocktail shaker filled with ice. Strain into a Highball glass and garnish with a lemon slice. Top up with soda, if desired.

RIP MURDOCK *"It looked like feeding time at the zoo. All you needed was money to start with and bicarbonate of soda to finish."*

DEAD RECKONING (1947)

War heroes Rip Murdock (Humphrey Bogart, below) and Johnny Drake (William Prince) are on a train to a Washington DC awards ceremony when Drake disappears. A confounded and curious Murdock pursues his pal, only to discover that he had once been convicted for murder, and joined the army under an assumed name. Drake is killed, leaving Murdock determined to hunt down his killer. He meets and falls in love with Coral Chandler (Lizabeth Scott, below) the wife of Drake's victim, whose answer to grieving is gin. "What do you do?" she asks. "Do you go on drinking Ramos Gin Fizzes?" Perhaps not a mourning drink *per se*, but most certainly an early evening one.

HUMORESQUE (1946)

If music be the food of love, play on, as they say. Named after the Dvorak composition performed in the film, *Humoresque* is a highly strung melodrama featuring Joan Crawford as Helen Wright (above), a wealthy and glamorous arts patron. Paul Boray (John Garfield, above), a promising violinist from the lower East Side, is her latest acquisition. Helen falls for her young prodigy, but is unable to win him over from his first love, music. In despair, she drowns her sorrows in an ocean of alcohol. The music is splendid: Isaac Stern provides the instrumental solos, and the realistic fingering and bowing was achieved through some ingenious sleight of hand.

HELEN TO PAUL *"Don't you like Martinis? They're an acquired taste – like Ravel."*

50 ML LONDON DRY GIN

FRESH LEMON JUICE

SUGAR SYRUP

SODA

SLICE OF LEMON

Pour the gin, a small shot of lemon juice and a dash of sugar syrup into a Highball glass filled with ice. Top up with soda, stir, and garnish with a slice of lemon.

TOM COLLINS

A drinks trolley by the pool; an afternoon dip and a refreshing Collins to take off the goosebumps. Tom is the best-known member of the Collins "cocktail" family, but the original was John – named after its inventor, and created back in late 19th century London at the Limmer's Hotel. The John Collins was made with Dutch gin, but today, this cocktail has been more or less replaced by the Tom Collins, which uses London Dry gin.

The Gimlet is another classic cocktail that combines simplicity with practicality, almost certainly named after a tool used for boring small holes. How it first came into being is less clear. Rose's Lime Cordial was invented by Lauchlan Rose, who began importing limes from the Caribbean in the 1860s. It seems possible that, like the Pink Gin, this cocktail was born on board a British naval ship, where the cordial would have been used to prevent scurvy.

GIMLET

50 ML GIN (OR VODKA)
25 ML ROSE'S LIME CORDIAL

Pour the gin or vodka into a cocktail shaker filled with ice; add the cordial to taste (two parts spirit to one part cordial is the norm). Shake sharply and strain into a frosted Martini glass, or serve over ice in a rocks glass.

FRANCESCA VON STEFFAN (SEATED)

"I devoured your last book, Harry."

HARRY STREET *"Well, I hope it didn't give you a bellyache."*

THE SNOWS OF KILIMANJARO (1952)

Dangerously ill and delirious with fever, Harry Street (Gregory Peck, below left) lies on the edge of death at the foot of Mount Kilimanjaro in Africa, where he is attended by his devoted wife, Helen (Susan Hayward). In his delirium, Street journeys back into his past as a roving writer, a life he thinks was less than successful. Flashbacks introduce Cynthia (Ava Gardner), the love Street lost during the Spanish Civil War. Parisian cafés, the Riviera and great vistas of Africa are all captured with superb cinematography. Based on a novel by Ernest Hemingway, the film was a great success – though not, it seems, appreciated by the Old Man himself.

NINOTCHKA (1939)

"I'm so happy! I'm so happy! Nobody can be so happy without being punished," says Ninotchka (Greta Garbo, above) in this fine comedy screenplay written by Billy Wilder. Ninotchka is a Russian commissar who has come to Paris to sell jewellery belonging to the grand duchess (Ina Claire) of the exiled White Russians. When the duchess' French boyfriend Count Léon (Melvyn Douglas) is brought in to stop the sale, he falls instead for Ninotchka, and eventually manages to break down her communist reserve with Champagne and Parisian life. The film pokes fun at both communism and capitalism, using a balance of romance and comedy.

NINOTCHKA *"I should hate to see our country endangered by my underwear!"*

40 ML RUSSIAN VODKA

20 ML KAHLUA

MARASCHINO CHERRY

Fill a rocks glass to the brim with ice. Pour in the vodka and the Kahlúa and garnish with a Maraschino cherry.

To make a White Russian, add 20ml of single cream to the recipe and float gently on top. Garnish with a stemmed cherry.

BLACK RUSSIAN

The Cold War may be over, but Poland and Russia are still at loggerheads over the origins of vodka; each claims this neutral and virtually tasteless spirit as its own. Beware, however: vodka more than makes up in effect what it lacks in personality. Limit your after dinner Black Russians – or be prepared to suffer the consequences!

Especially popular in the 18th century, the Flip was a sweetened hot drink built upon beer or ale, combined with (most often) rum, egg and spices. A traditional Flip would have been served in a mug, but later it became fashionable to offer it cold in a small goblet. The name comes from flipping the ingredients back and forth to achieve a thoroughly mixed, smooth texture; the Brandy Flip is one of the more popular versions.

BRANDY

FLIP ·············

50 ML BRANDY

1 EGG

1 DASH OF SUGAR SYRUP

Stir all the ingredients thoroughly in a mixing glass filled with ice. Strain into a wine glass.

OTTO KRINGELEIN *"Life is wonderful, but it is very dangerous. If you have the courage to live it, it's marvellous."*

GRAND HOTEL (1932)

In 1932, MGM packed the cast of *Grand Hotel* with the studio's biggest stars: Greta Garbo as the dancer Grusinskaya; John Barrymore as Baron Felix von Gaigern, her lover and a jewel thief; Lionel Barrymore as Otto Kringelein (below), a dying man taken to drink; Joan Crawford as Flaemmchen (below) and Wallace Beery as General Director Preysing. The result: an Oscar award for Best Picture and a box-office hit. Dr Otternschlag (played by Lewis Stone) bemoans, "Grand Hotel: always the same. People come, people go. Nothing ever happens." But what actually happens is that romance and humility triumph over adversity in Berlin.

30 ML BRANDY

30 ML DARK RUM

1 EGG

1 TEASPOON OF SUGAR

MILK

FRESHLY GRATED NUTMEG

Pour all the ingredients except the milk into a cocktail shaker filled with ice and shake sharply. Strain into a rocks glass. Top up with milk and stir. Sprinkle with freshly grated nutmeg.

EGG NOG

Egg Nog is considered an essential part of Christmas festivities. In the American South, it is served mainly as a hot "cocktail", using bourbon in place of brandy and rum. Whatever its temperature, Egg Nog is primarily a Flip with milk or cream added. The name probably comes from "noggin" – a small mug used to serve Flips.

THE MAN WHO CAME TO DINNER (1941)

The Man Who Came To Dinner is Sheridan Whiteside (Monty Woolley, above), a radio celebrity whose insults would turn milk sour. On a lecture tour of the American Midwest with his assistant Maggie Cutler (Bette Davis), he slips on some ice at the home of the Stanleys (Billie Burke and Grant Mitchell) and breaks his leg, staying on as a guest for the next month. Whiteside interferes with the lives of all around him, including Miss Cutler, who falls in love with Richard Travis (Bert Jefferson). The only thing that doesn't freeze beneath his icy touch is the Egg Nog.

WHITESIDE TO HIS NURSE *"Don't stand there, Miss Preen. You look like a frozen custard."*

Like the Kir Royale, the Buck's Fizz is a popular drink for weddings and receptions. Invented at the beginning of the 1920s and accredited to the Buck's Club in London, the drink was "top hat" among the flapper set. As popular as the Buck's Fizz, the Mimosa is often served in exactly the same way, although some variations will call for a splash of Grand Marnier. Both drinks also make great accompaniments to brunch.

BUCK'S FIZZ

DRY CHAMPAGNE
FRESH ORANGE JUICE

Make sure that your ingredients are well chilled for this cocktail. Half fill a Champagne flute with Champagne. Top up with fresh orange juice and stir gently.

To make a Mimosa, create a Buck's Fizz and add a dash of Orange Curaçao or Grand Marnier.

DALE TREMONT *"What is this strange power you have over horses?"*

JERRY TRAVERS *"Horsepower?"*

TOP HAT (1935)

Who needs a plot when you have Fred Astaire and Ginger Rogers (both below) tapping away to songs by Irving Berlin? Magical dance routines – especially "Isn't This a Lovely Day?" – and a fine art deco backdrop ensured that *Top Hat* became a smash at the box office. The story-line features a romantic misunderstanding, and a good dose of comedy ensues as the charming and witty Jerry Travers (Astaire) pursues an exasperated Dale Tremont (Rogers) through London and Venice. Audiences and critics alike adored it, and it won awards for Best Song ("Cheek to Cheek") and Best Dance Direction ("Top Hat, White Tie and Tails") at the Oscars.

At the end of the day, getting ready for bed or when you're just feeling down, there's no better comfort cure than a Hot Toddy. Administered frequently, it can revive the spirits of even the most downtrodden. The name "toddy" appears to have come to England from India, where the toddy palm was tapped for its sap and fermented to make palm wine.

·········· HOT TODDY

CAT ON A HOT TIN ROOF (1958)

A triumph on stage, Tennessee Williams' *Cat On A Hot Tin Roof* also landed on its feet with the screen version, making top dollar for MGM in 1958. Paul Newman and Elizabeth Taylor star as Brick and Maggie Pollitt (left), a husband and wife suffering marital strife. The heart of the problem is Brick's reluctance to sleep with his wife due to his latent homosexuality – an issue explored more deeply in the play, but only insinuated in the film. Burl Ives plays Brick's father, Big Daddy, a wealthy southern plantation owner who is dying of cancer. As if that weren't trouble enough, Brick's brother Gooper (Jack Carson), and sister-in-law Mae (Madeleine Sherwood) try to destroy the status Brick holds with Big Daddy.

50 ML SCOTCH WHISKY

FRESH LEMON JUICE

1 LEMON

1 TABLESPOON HONEY

GROUND CINNAMON

CINNAMON STICK

5 CLOVES

BOILING WATER

- *Pour the whisky and honey into a heat-proof rocks glass. Add half a glass of boiling water and stir vigorously. Spear five cloves into the skin of a lemon slice and place into the glass; add a sprinkling of cinnamon and a large dash of fresh lemon juice. Stir again and garnish with a cinnamon stick.*

MAGGIE TO BRICK *"I'm not living with you. We occupy the same cage, that's all."*

The Rickey is a delightfully delicious drink that refreshes even the driest of throats. Closely related to the Sour, Collins and Fizz, it is easy to make with any spirit or liqueur you desire. The Gin Rickey should be made with a top-quality gin in order to get a perfect balance of fresh, crisp flavours.

GIN RICKEY ·····

50 ML GIN

FRESH LIME JUICE

SUGAR SYRUP

SODA

LIME WEDGE

Pour the gin, a large dash of fresh lime juice and a large dash of sugar syrup into a Highball glass filled with ice. Top up with soda, and garnish with a lime wedge.

Originally this was just the Alexander Cocktail, made with gin. This version was developed as an after-dinner drink and became the more popular of the two. The combination of brandy (a superb *digestif* in its own right), cream and *crème de cacao* helps settle the stomach after even the richest of meals.

BRANDY ALEXANDER

40 ML BRANDY

20 ML WHITE CREME DE CACAO

20 ML DARK CREME DE CACAO

FRESH SINGLE CREAM

GROUND NUTMEG

Pour all of the ingredients and a dash of fresh cream into a cocktail shaker filled with ice. Shake sharply; strain into a frosted Martini glass. Garnish with a sprinkle of ground nutmeg.

50 ML BRANDY

25 ML WHITE CREME DE MENTHE

Pour the brandy and crème de menthe into a cocktail shaker filled with ice. Shake sharply and strain into a frosted Martini glass.

STINGER

In *High Society* – the musical version of *The Philadelphia Story* – CK Dexter Haven (Bing Crosby) explains to Tracy Lord (Grace Kelly) how the Stinger got its name. "It's a Stinger," Haven says simply. "It removes the sting." It is also an excellent after-dinner drink that truly aids the digestion.

30 ML DARK RUM

30 ML BRANDY

1 EGG, SEPARATED

1 BARSPOON SUGAR

BOILING WATER

GROUND NUTMEG

Beat the egg white and yolk separately, then mix them together in a heat-resistant wine glass. Add remaining ingredients to the egg mixture and top it up with boiling water. Sprinkle with ground nutmeg.

TOM AND JERRY

This is no cartoon character concoction. It takes its name from the great inventor of many cocktails, Professor Jerry Thomas, who created the drink back in the mid-1800s. It's ideal at any time, day or night, but is probably at its most enjoyable when sipped in front of a roaring fire.

FROM HERE TO ETERNITY

DRINKS FOR ALL OCCASIONS

Hollywood, in its heyday, had sumptuous settings and tropical locations for its films – and the cocktails consumed on location were just as exotic. There was the sweet charm of southern plantations, captured in fragrant Juleps or a Planter's Punch, whereas Manhattan madness was reflected in mind-numbing Zombies. Expatriate Americanos were imbibed on the Continent, while cinema audiences learned all about the wicked pleasures of rum by watching various stars cavort in island paradises. Like any good Hollywood fantasy, a well-stocked cocktail cabinet allows you to transform an ordinary summer's day, an evening out, or virtually any occasion into a truly extraordinary event.

25 ML CAMPARI

25 ML SWEET VERMOUTH

SODA

SLICE OF ORANGE

Add ice to a Highball glass.
Pour in the spirits and top up
with soda. Stir and garnish
with a slice of orange.

AMERICANO

The Americano is an easy cocktail to make for kicking off an afternoon party under the blazing sun. Created in Italy, the homeland of Campari, it became popular among visiting Americans during the Prohibition era. For those who would like to step up to something stronger, simply add a little gin and the Americano becomes a Negroni. First imbibed by Count Camillo Negroni in Florence during the Roaring Twenties, this bitter libation might just benefit from a splash of soda to help it along.

THE ROMAN SPRING OF MRS STONE (1962)

Another film adaptation of a Tennessee Williams'
work, this time based on his only novel. *The Roman
Spring of Mrs Stone* stars Vivien Leigh as Karen
Stone (above), a widowed, middle-aged actress who
forsakes her fading career to move to Rome. Almost
immediately, she finds a companion in the form of

gigolo Paolo di Leo (Warren Beatty, above, left), who
wastes no time in exploiting her for financial gain.
Lotte Lenya plays Contessa Magda Terribili-Gonzales,
the mastermind behind Karen and Paolo's romantic
rendezvous, who eventually draws him back to help
a young actress, Barbera Bingham (Jill St John). Mrs
Stone is devastated, and spring quickly turns to fall.

BARBERA BINGHAM *"I never saw you on the stage. Isn't that terrible?"*

KAREN STONE *"Not at all. I've never seen you on the screen."*

The Pimm's Cocktail will be found wherever followers of polo, lawn tennis or cricket congregate. A Gin Sling at heart, Pimm's is one of the few pre-mixed drinks that has stood the test of time. First made in 1840, the Pimm's No 1 Cup (six eventually evolved, based on different spirits) is renowned around the globe. A little stronger than the Americano, this is a delightful drink to while away an afternoon – of plotting or otherwise.

·············· PIMM'S COCKTAIL

50 ML PIMM'S NO 1 CUP

LEMONADE OR 7-UP

CUCUMBER

MIXED FRUIT TO TASTE

SPRIG OF MINT

Pour Pimm's over ice into a Highball glass and add the lemonade, leaving ample room for the fruit. Then add a sliver of cucumber peel, a slice of orange, lemon and strawberry and a sprig of mint. Serve with a straw and a swizzle stick.

DOUBLE INDEMNITY (1944)

From the moment they met, it was murder! Fred MacMurray (right) sheds the shackles of niceness to give the performance of his career as Walter Neff, an insurance salesman lured by greed and passion into intrigue beyond his control. This compelling *film noir* adaptation (by Billy Wilder and Raymond Chandler) of James Cain's short story opens with a wounded Neff confessing his crime on a dictaphone. In flashbacks the story unfolds – Phyllis Dietrichson (Barbara Stanwyck, right) has lured Neff into a fraudulent life insurance scam. Into the frame walks Barton Keyes (played by Edward G Robinson), the claims investigator. Riveting from beginning to end, *Double Indemnity* is one of the finest suspense and cold-blooded crime films to come out of Hollywood.

WALTER NEFF *"I never knew that murder could smell like honeysuckle."*

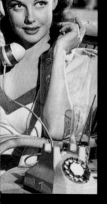

Like so many cocktails, no one knows the origins of the Mint Julep for certain – particularly as the word "julep" is a corruption of Persian "guleb", a medicinal drink of syrup, flavourings and water. How it took root in America's Deep South is anybody's guess, but it is thought to have been introduced to Europe by a Captain Marryatt, a British skipper who referred to it as "one of the most delightful and insinuating potions that ever was invented".

MINT JULEP

50ML BOURBON

5 SPRIGS OF FRESH MINT

1 WHITE SUGAR CUBE

SODA (OR WATER)

- *Muddle the mint and sugar together with the bourbon and a dash of soda in a rocks glass until the sugar has dissolved and the flavour of the mint has been extracted. Fill the glass with crushed ice and stir. Garnish with a mint sprig and serve with straws.*

WHITESIDE *"He's just your dish, my dear."*
LORRAINE "LOU" SHELDON
"I'll take the first train tomorrow morning. Good looking, too, huh? I can hardly wait."

THE MAN WHO CAME TO DINNER (1941)

Acquiring the rights to Kaufman and Hart's hit Broadway comedy cost a mint. Warner Brothers optioned the play at the request of Bette Davis, who wished to star in it, with John Barrymore at her side. Barrymore, however, kept swallowing his lines and was replaced by Monty Woolley, who had performed the role of Sheridan Whiteside on stage. The film portrays a cast of characters based loosely on real-life celebrities Alexander Woollcott (Whiteside, played by Woolley), a Marx Brother (Banjo, played by Jimmy Durante) and Noël Coward (Beverly Carlton, played by Reginald Gardiner). Ann Sheridan plays the part of actress Lorraine Sheldon (below) famously.

PHANTOM SUBMARINE (1941)

In this seagoing story of intrigue, Anita Louise plays the part of Madeleine Nielson (above), a newspaper reporter recruited by the navy to investigate the mysterious marine activities of the *Retriever*, a treasure-hunting vessel searching for sunken gold. A suspicious explosion sends the boat into port, where a wealthy foreigner, Henri Jerome (John Tyrell II, above, centre) pays for repairs. He prevents Nielson from rejoining the ship, but she is rescued by Paul Sinclair (Bruce Bennett). Meanwhile, Jerome has sent a submarine to capture the *Retriever*. With suspense throughout, and fine underwater photography, *Phantom Submarine* will appeal to all salty dogs.

HENRI JEROME *"Some cooling drinks? You must be thirsty."*
MADELEINE NIELSON *"We're burning up, but it's with curiosity."*

- 50 ML VODKA
- CRANBERRY JUICE
- FRESH GRAPEFRUIT JUICE
- LIME WEDGE

Pour the vodka into a Highball glass filled with ice. Fill the glass 3/4 full with cranberry juice and top up with grapefruit juice. Garnish with a lime wedge.

To make a Salty Dog, hold the cranberry juice. Pour the vodka into a salt-rimmed rocks glass full of ice (salt the rim by rubbing the edge with lemon juice, then dipping rim in salt). Top with grapefruit juice and serve without garnish.

SEA BREEZE

This cocktail gets its name from the cooling winds that come off the ocean, a phenomenon that occurs when the ocean is cooler than the land. Just like the fickle direction of those winds, the Sea Breeze has changed. Back in the 1920s and '30s, it was gin-based; since then, it has become a favourite vodka cocktail.

Several members of the cocktail family have taken their names from the tool chest: the Gimlet, the Ice Pick and (obliquely) the Rusty Nail, to cite just a few. Yet how a vodka- and orange-based cocktail got a name like Screwdriver requires a stretch of the imagination. Supposedly, it was devised in the 1940s by an American who found himself without a swizzle stick and turned to his utility belt for assistance.

SCREWDRIVER

FROM HERE TO ETERNITY (1953)

This movie classic is remembered mainly for the lovemaking scene on the beach between Sgt Milton Warden and Karen Holmes, the wife of Warden's superior officer (Burt Lancaster and Deborah Kerr, left). *From Here To Eternity* allowed both Montgomery Clift (as Robert E Lee Prewitt) and Frank Sinatra (as Angelo Maggio) to give masterful performances. Prewitt is a GI posted to the Honolulu barracks who refuses to join the company boxing team. As a result, he is given assignments designed to destroy his morale. His only friend is Maggio, who also feels the wrath of the sadistic Sgt Judson (played by Ernest Borgnine). Sultry performances by Donna Reed as a "hostess" and Kerr as the adulterous wife make the screen sizzle – from here to eternity.

50 ML VODKA
FRESH ORANGE JUICE
SLICE OF ORANGE

Pour the vodka into a Highball glass filled with ice. Top up with orange juice and garnish with a slice of orange.

SGT WARDEN *"It's not confidence, ma'am; it's honesty. I just hate to see a beautiful woman going all to waste."*

CASABLANCA (1942)

Casablanca was a hit from the first day it opened, three weeks, coincidentally, after the Allies reached the real Casablanca. Its mix of romance, intrigue and nostalgia, shaken up with a little despair and corruption, created a heat throughout the film that only made audiences thirsty for more.

"I came to Casablanca for the waters," says Rick Blaine (Humphrey Bogart). "Waters, what waters? We're in the desert," replies Captain Louis Renault (Claude Rains). Bogart quips: "I was misinformed." Winner of Best Picture, Director and Screenplay Oscars, the image of Bogart and Bergman is forever etched in movie buffs' memories "As Time Goes By".

RICK BLAINE *"Of all the gin joints in all the towns in the world, she walks into mine."*

50 ML GIN

25 ML FRESH LEMON JUICE

SUGAR SYRUP

CHERRY HEERING

SLICE OF LEMON

STEMMED CHERRY

Pour the gin, lemon juice and a dash of sugar syrup into a cocktail shaker. Shake sharply, then strain into a sling glass filled with crushed ice. Muddle the mixture using a spoon, then add a float of Cherry Heering. Garnish with a slice of lemon and a stemmed cherry, and serve with straws.

SINGAPORE SLING

"Everybody comes to Rick's." They come to escape and they come to drink: a Cointreau perhaps, or for those seeking to quench their thirst in the desert heat, a Singapore Sling. The original Singapore Sling was created by Ngiam Tong Boon – bartender at the legendary Raffles Hotel. This version employs a variation of Ngiam's first recipe.

Sloppy Joe's, El Floridita and La Bodeguita del Medio are Havana bars renowned both for the drinks they invented and the famous names who imbibed them. Ernest Hemingway was just one of the celebrities who frequented all three establishments, but La Bodeguita was a particular favourite, not least because writers could buy drinks on credit there. One of these was the Mojito – a sure cure for writer's block.

MOJITO

OUR MAN IN HAVANA (1959)

Based on the novel by Graham Greene, *Our Man in Havana* puts a different spin on spy movies. Jim Wormold, played by Sir Alec Guinness (left), is a vacuum cleaner salesman in Havana who gets absorbed by accident into the British Secret Service. Hoping to make more money by the misadventure, Wormold creates a series of fictional characters so that he can feed information about them back to headquarters. Assisted in London by "95200" (Sir Noël Coward, far left) and "C", the chief of security (Sir Ralph Richardson), Wormold seems to be pulling it off, until a certain Dr Hasselbacher (Burl Ives) causes the web of deceit to unravel – with serious consequences.

50 ML GOLDEN RUM
DASH OF FRESH LIME JUICE
DASH OF SUGAR SYRUP
4 FRESH MINT LEAVES
SODA

Place mint leaves into a Highball glass and add rum; muddle vigorously until the mint flavour is extracted. Add shaved ice, lime juice and sugar syrup to taste. Stir and top up with soda. Serve with straws.

95200 *"I'm in charge of the Caribbean network."*
JIM WORMOLD *"It sounds like the Secret Service."*
95200 *"So the novelists call it."*

TO HAVE AND HAVE NOT (1944)

Harry "Steve" Morgan (Humphrey Bogart) runs a hire boat together with hard-drinking Eddie (Walter Brennan) in Nazi-occupied Martinique. It isn't long before Morgan gets involved with the French Resistance and sultry singer Marie "Slim" Browning (Lauren Bacall, above). The love scenes are legendary, probably because the palpable magnetism between the stars was fuelled by an off-screen romance. Gripping action, great dialogue (by William Faulkner and Jules Furthman) and songs from Bacall make *To Have and Have Not* as classic as the Daiquiri itself.

"SLIM" BROWNING *"You know how to whistle, don't you, Steve? You just put your lips together and blow."*

50 ML LIGHT OR GOLDEN RUM

20 ML FRESH LIME JUICE

2 ½ TEASPOONS SUGAR SYRUP

- *Pour all of the ingredients into an ice-filled cocktail shaker. Shake sharply and strain into a frosted Martini glass.*

DAIQUIRI

Humphrey Bogart's character in *To Have and Have Not* was based on Joe Russell, owner of "Sloppy Joe's" bar in Havana. The bar was famous for its regular and frozen Daiquiris, which, Ernest Hemingway wrote, "felt, as you drank them, the way downhill glacier-skiing feels running through powder snow...". Said to have been named for a small town on the east coast of Cuba, the drink was created at the end of the 19th century by an American engineer called Jennings Cox.

30 ML BRANDY

30 ML RUM

MILK

WHITE SUGAR TO TASTE

GRATED NUTMEG

Stir the brandy and rum together in a mixing glass filled with ice, then strain into a rocks glass. Top up with milk, add sugar to taste and sprinkle with grated nutmeg.

MILK PUNCH

How to make a Milk Punch, courtesy of *Guys and Dolls*. "At night they put a kind of preservative in it," says Sky Masterson. "That's interesting. What do they use?" asks Sarah Brown. "Bacardi." "Doesn't that have alcohol in it?" "Well, just enough to stop the milk from turning sour." This drink is popular in Cuba, but found real fame in New Orleans.

GUYS AND DOLLS (1955)

Songs and sin add up to a lavish Sam Goldwyn musical. Nathan Detroit (Frank Sinatra) runs a floating crap game that is temporarily homeless. To raise money, he bets Sky Masterson (Marlon Brando, above) that he can't persuade any girl named by Detroit to go with him to Havana. Sky takes him on, only to find that Detroit has chosen missionary Sarah Brown (Jean Simmons, above). He convinces her to go by promising a full congregation for her mission, and Sarah quickly takes to the milk drinks Sky orders for her. ("That Bacardi flavouring certainly does make a difference.") In Havana, against all odds, they fall in love, and being saved takes on a whole new meaning.

SARAH BROWN *"This is a tasty milkshake."*

A longer version of the Daiquiri, the Mai Tai claims to be "the best" – at least, that's the literal translation of its Tahitian name. Invented by Victor Bergeron, the man responsible for the Trader Vic's chain of Polynesian-themed bars and restaurants, the Mai Tai first appeared in 1944 in California, when Bergeron allegedly created "something special" for some Tahitian friends who were visiting the United States.

MAI TAI

- 50 ML DEMERARA RUM
- FRESH LEMON JUICE
- FRESH LIME JUICE
- ORANGE CURACAO
- APRICOT BRANDY
- ORGEAT SYRUP
- ANGOSTURA BITTERS
- PINEAPPLE JUICE
- 2 MINT LEAVES
- SLICE OF PINEAPPLE
- SPRIG OF MINT

Pour the rum and large dashes of lemon juice, lime juice and orgeat syrup into a cocktail shaker filled with cracked ice. Add small shots of apricot brandy and orange curaçao, two dashes of Angostura bitters, a large measure of pineapple juice and two mint leaves. Shake the mixture sharply; pour into a rocks glass. Garnish with a slice of pineapple and a sprig of mint.

BLUE HAWAII (1961)

The picture-postcard South Pacific provides the setting for this Elvis Presley extravaganza. Presley plays Chad Gates (below), returning home to Hawaii after a brief stint in the army. Son of pineapple tycoon Fred Gates (Roland Winters, below), he decides not to follow in his father's footsteps. The tropical location provides ample opportunity for Elvis to strut his stuff in bathing trunks and enjoy romantic interludes with Maile Duval (Joan Blackman, below). The King's fans will also enjoy a musical score that includes such hits as "I Can't Help Falling in Love".

SARAH TO FRED GATES *"Careful, Daddy: those Mai Tais can be mighty powerful."*

Twelve Oaks, a barbecue, all the neighbours and a warm, sunny, Southern afternoon is the perfect setting for a Planter's Punch. It hails from the sugar plantations of Jamaica, and first credit for this drink is given to Frank Myers, who opened a rum distillery in the late 19th century. In truth, however, variations on the Planter's Punch theme have been around since rum was first invented back in the 1700s.

····· PLANTER'S PUNCH

50 ML MYERS DARK RUM

25 ML FRESH LIME JUICE

SUGAR SYRUP

ANGOSTURA BITTERS

SODA

LIME WEDGE

- *Pour the rum and lime juice into a cocktail shaker filled with ice, add a large dash of sugar syrup and two dashes Angostura bitters. Shake and strain into a Highball glass filled with ice. Top up with soda and garnish with a lime wedge.*

GONE WITH THE WIND (1939)

Glorious scenes of plantation life are soon shattered in cinema's best-loved epic, based on Margaret Mitchell's only novel. The role of Scarlett O'Hara became the most sought after in movie history: Paulette Goddard, Bette Davis, Joan Crawford, Jean Harlow, Carole Lombard and Tallulah Bankhead were all in the running, along with countless unknowns. Vivien Leigh (right) was finally chosen to play the headstrong Southern belle, whose scenes with a dashing Rhett Butler (Clark Gable) are famous for their punchy dialogue. What fans didn't realise was that Gable's breath made Leigh's role one of the most unenviable on earth.

ARA *"After all, tomorrow is another day."*

If Holly Golightly was intent on leaving the party "very drunk indeed", then the Zombie was the right drink to choose for the occasion. Everything except the kitchen sink can be found in this drink, which was invented by Don Beach, a Hollywood restaurant owner, in 1934. Supposedly created as a hangover cure, it's sure to do the reverse. As a "corpse reviver", however, it may well raise the living dead.

ZOMBIE

BREAKFAST AT TIFFANY'S (1961)

"Top banana in the shock department" is how party girl Holly Golightly (Audrey Hepburn, left) describes herself. This free spirit always knows how to throw a *soirée*, but all is not what it seems: her glamour and sophistication hide a more sombre past. "She's a phoney," her agent points out, "but a real phoney." *Breakfast at Tiffany's* is based on a novella by Truman Capote, who originally envisaged Marilyn Monroe as the lead. George Peppard charms as Paul "Fred" Varjak, the clean-cut writer who befriends, and eventually falls for, the hapless Holly.

- 20 ML LIGHT RUM
- 20 ML GOLDEN RUM
- 20 ML JAMAICAN RUM
- 20 ML OVER-PROOF RUM
- FRESH LIME JUICE
- FRESH PASSION-FRUIT JUICE
- FRESH PINEAPPLE JUICE
- SUGAR SYRUP

Pour the frist three rums into a cocktail shaker and add a large dash of lime juice. To this, add two large dashes of both other juices and a dash of sugar syrup (to taste). Shake the mixture sharply and strain into a Highball glass filled with ice. Float a measure of over-proof rum on top and finish with any elaborate garnish.

HOLLY GOLIGHTLY *"Promise me one thing: don't take me home until I'm drunk – very drunk indeed."*

There are few brand names better known than Bacardi in the drinks world. Coca-Cola is one of them. The Cuba Libre is the result of these two brands coming together to create the Highball, "rum and coke". First made by an American soldier in Cuba in the early 20th century, the drink has risen in popularity ever since.

CUBA LIBRE

50 ML WHITE OR GOLDEN RUM
JUICE OF 1 LIME
COCA-COLA

Pour the rum and cola into a Highball glass filled with ice. Cut the lime into quarters and squeeze into the glass. Stir and serve.

The most tropical of exotic cocktails, the Piña Colada combines the ubiquitous pineapple of Hawaii with coconut. Almost a dessert in a glass, the Piña Colada must be served chilled and smooth. Its origins are unclear, but the word *piña* hails from Mexico and refers to the pineapple-shaped core of the maguey cactus.

PINA COLADA

Pour all the ingredients into a blender, add one scoop of crushed ice and blend on a high speed for one minute. Pour into a large colada glass, and garnish with a slice of pineapple.

50 ML GOLDEN RUM
COCONUT CREAM
PINEAPPLE JUICE (OR FRESH
PINEAPPLE CHUNKS)
SLICE OF PINEAPPLE

50 ML GOLD TEQUILA

FRESH ORANGE JUICE

GRENADINE

SLICE OF ORANGE

Pour the tequila into a Highball glass filled with ice, top up with orange juice and add a sunken float of grenadine. Garnish with a slice of orange and serve with a straw.

TEQUILA SUNRISE

Tequila can be traced back to the Aztecs, who fermented the juice of the agave cactus. Fresh agave juice is made into a beer-like liquid called *pulque*, which in turn is distilled to produce a strong white spirit. Tequila may only be called Tequila if it is made from the blue agave cactus. From any other variety, it is called Mezcal.

50 ML GOLD TEQUILA

25 ML FRESH LIME JUICE

20 ML TRIPLE SEC

(OR COINTREAU)

Rub the rim of a Margarita glass with a wedge of lime and dip the rim into a saucer of fine salt. Place all the ingredients into a cocktail shaker filled with ice. Shake well and strain into the glass.

MARGARITA

The Margarita is by far the best-known Tequila cocktail, and the one with the longest history. Most drinks legends place its birth in America's Old West, during the Gold Rush days. According to the most romantic version of the story, a bartender in one of the frontier towns created it in honour of his "gal", who shielded him from a bullet, then died in his arms.

REMEMBER LAST NIGHT?

DRINKS FOR THE DAY AFTER THE NIGHT BEFORE

All good things must come to an end, but while you can always walk out of a bad film, you simply can't walk away from a bad hangover. Yet give the filmmakers their due: Hollywood may have laughed frequently at the effects of excessive drinking on screen, but its scripts also offered all sorts of cures for the suffering.

In The Philadelphia Story, for instance, Uncle Willie suggests a tonic "said to pop the pennies off the eyelids of dead Irishmen" – sadly, it doesn't seem to have the same effect on the living. Other concoctions include the dubious-sounding Prairie Oyster and Corpse Reviver, but the tried and tested favourite – for directors and ticket holders alike – remains the Bloody Mary.

REMEMBER LAST NIGHT? (1935)

Adapted from the novel *Hangover Murders* by Adam Hobhouse, *Remember Last Night?* is a comedy thriller directed by James Whale. Recently married couple Tony and Carlotta Milburn (Robert Young and Constance Cummings, above, far right) get together with their closest friends to celebrate six months of wedded bliss. The party lasts through the night, but a new day dawns upon the corpse of one of the guests. Suffering from over-indulgence and subsequent short-term memory loss, the remaining party-goers are incapable of assisting the detective in charge, Danny Harrison (Edward Arnold). A hypnotist is hired to recreate the crime scene, but before he is able to reveal the murderer's identity, he, too, is killed. What happens next? Funny; I can't seem to remember...

CARLOTTA *"Oh, what's going to happen?"*
TONY *"Almost anything, to any one
of us... I'll never take another
drink as long as I live!"*

30 ML BRANDY
20 ML SWEET VERMOUTH
20 ML CALVADOS
ORANGE ZEST

*Fill a mixing glass with ice and add the
ingredients. Stir the mixture gently using a spoon
until the mixing glass frosts and its contents are
blended. Strain into a frosted Martini glass and
garnish with a strip of orange zest.*

CORPSE REVIVER

If "Zombie" best describes your waking state the day after the night before, then it might
be wise to follow Harry Craddock's advice on the Corpse Reviver – "to be taken before
11AM, or whenever steam and energy are needed". But beware: created by Frank Meier
at the Ritz bar in Paris, this stiff bracer may well bring back rememberances of things past!

DON JUAN QUILLIGAN (1945)

William Bendix plays the role of Patrick "Don Juan" Quilligan (below, left), a Hudson River barge captain. Quilligan holds a romantic idealisation of women that is so out of proportion he ends up being married to two at once. Fortunately, each wife lives on opposite banks of the Hudson; hence "Don Juan" is married to Marjorie Mossrock (Joan Blondell) in Brooklyn and Lucy (Mary Treen) in Utica. When things get out of hand, his best friend Mac Denny, (played by Phil Silvers, below, centre), fakes a murder/suicide so that his bigamous friend can escape troubled married life – only to end up serving his time behind bars.

If the idea of having to down a raw egg yolk steeped in vinegar and Worcestershire sauce isn't sufficient aversion therapy, then the name of this drink certainly is – a prairie oyster is the term given to a bull's testicle. In spite of all this, many swear by this cocktail as a cure for hangover headaches and wobbly stomachs – *if* it's to be drunk, down it in one. Perhaps it's better not to know its inventor...

PRAIRIE OYSTER

- 40 ML COGNAC
- 1 EGG YOLK
- 1 BARSPOON MALT VINEGAR
- 2 DASHES OF TABASCO SAUCE
- 1 BARSPOON WORCESTERSHIRE SAUCE
- SALT AND PEPPER

Place the egg yolk, unbroken, into a Margarita glass. Gently pour in the rest of the ingredients without breaking the yolk. Drink it down in one – and pray.

MAC DENNY *"Egg? Let's stir it a little: I think that'll do."*

Of all the reviver cocktails the Bloody Mary is the most versatile and most palatable. Back in the early 1920s, at Harry's New York Bar in Paris, "Pete" Petiot mixed the spicy ingredients of the Bloody Mary for the first time. Whether it was really named after the Tudor Queen who butchered protestants is unclear, but the only "blood" in this drink comes from tomato juice – and you'd be hard-pressed not to like it.

... BLOODY MARY

THE GIRL CAN'T HELP IT (1956)

For hard-drinking press agent Tom Miller (Tom Ewell, left), the prospect of hyping gangster's moll Gerry Jordan (Jayne Mansfield, left) could end bloodily – especially when Gerry says of her boyfriend's casino: "Most of his best friends were killed there. Don't worry: he's changed the carpets". Luckily, the generously endowed Gerry saves Miller's skin and provides her own hangover cure into the bargain. This is an undemanding but hilarious pick-me-up of a movie, with great visual gags and gentle ribbing at the expense of the rock 'n' roll boom. Look out for Fats Domino, Little Richard, The Platters, Gene Vincent, Eddie Cochran and a ghostly cocktail *chanteuse*, Julie London, who (as herself) gives a haunting rendition of "Cry Me a River".

50 ML VODKA

TOMATO JUICE

SPICE MIX:

- 2 LARGE DASHES EACH OF TABASCO AND WORCESTERSHIRE SAUCE
- PINCH CELERY SALT
- PINCH CRACKED BLACK PEPPER
- 1 DASH OF FRESH LEMON JUICE
- 1 TEASPOON HORSERADISH SAUCE

SLICE OF LEMON

CELERY STICK

Blend ingredients for spice mix together in a mixing glass. Pour vodka into a Highball glass filled with ice, add tomato juice and spice mix and stir vigorously. Garnish with a lemon slice and a celery stick.

GERRY JORDAN TO TOM MILLER *"I think you need this... I made them for my father; he drank a lot – tried to forget my mother..."*

Elsewhere, the night deepened into silence and rest. But here, the brutal din of cheap music – booze – hate – lust – made a devil's carnival.

40 ML SCOTCH WHISKY

50 ML SINGLE CREAM

3 BARSPOONS HONEY

Pour all of the ingredients into a cocktail shaker filled with cracked ice. Strain into a Martini glass.

HAIR OF THE DOG

Over-indulgence can result in sheer hell, as *Underworld* mobster Bull Weed knows only too well. Yet unlike most of us who take one too many, Weed has not just a hangover, but a forthcoming hanging to fear: his own! If the threat of the gallows doesn't clear the head, then a little hair of the dog might just loosen the noose...

UNDERWORLD (1927)

Ben Hecht's first foray into screenwriting. *Underworld* is based upon his observations of Chicago gangster life during Prohibition. For his efforts, Hecht won the first-ever academy award for Best Original Screenplay. As its title suggests, the film takes place in the underworld haunts of gangster-land. Bull Weed (George Bancroft, above) is the ruling gangster, whose girlfriend "Feathers" (Evelyn Brent, above) is being coveted by his arch-rival, Buck Mulligan (Fred Kohler). A down-and-out lawyer (Clive Brook) known as "Rolls Royce" is hauled out of the gutter and cleaned up to become the brains behind Weed's brawn. Shrouded throughout in darkness, the silence of this film speaks volumes for its time.

Despite the renowned revelry of numerous Hollywood stars, relatively few cocktails honour idols of the silver screen. While Mary Pickford had a rum-based drink named after her, by far the most famous is this non-alcoholic concoction named after that most wholesome of child stars, Shirley Temple.

..... SHIRLEY TEMPLE

GRENADINE

GINGER ALE (OR 7-UP)

MARASCHINO CHERRY

Pour the ginger ale into a Highball glass filled with ice. Add the Grenadine to taste and stir. Garnish with a Maraschino cherry.

As popular as its alcoholic sister, the Bloody Mary, the Virgin Mary is everything you could want a Bloody Mary to be but without the vodka. Not, perhaps, a drink for any time of day, it is most suited as a morning-after brunch accompaniment, when the hangover isn't quite so desperate as it sometimes is.

TOMATO JUICE

2 LARGE DASHES

WORCESTERSHIRE SAUCE

2 LARGE DASHES TABASCO SAUCE

PINCH CELERY SALT

PINCH OF CRACKED BLACK PEPPER

1 DASH OF FRESH LEMON JUICE

1 TEASPOON HORSERADISH SAUCE

SLICE OF LEMON

CELERY STICK

VIRGIN MARY

Almost fill a Highball glass with tomato juice and ice. Blend rest of ingredients well in a mixing glass, then add to tomato juice and stir vigorously. Garnish with a lemon slice and a celery stick.

·············· ROY ROGERS

GRENADINE

COCA-COLA

MARASCHINO CHERRY

Pour the Coca-Cola into a Highball glass filled with ice. Add the grenadine to taste and stir. Garnish with a Maraschino cherry.

While he didn't achieve such international status as Shirley Temple, clean-living cowboy star Roy Rogers found enough fame among American fans to merit his own non-alcoholic cocktail. Basically a Shirley Temple made with Coca-Cola instead of ginger ale, its dark colour lends it a slightly more masculine appearance.

PUSSYFOOT COCKTAIL

Shake all of the ingredients in a cocktail shaker filled with ice. Strain into a rocks glass. Garnish with a stemmed cherry.

25 ML FRESH LIME JUICE

25 ML FRESH LEMON JUICE

25 ML FRESH ORANGE JUICE

DASH OF GRENADINE

STEMMED CHERRY

If, like the proverbial cat, you want to land on your feet, then look no further than the Pussyfoot Cocktail. A perfect choice for designated drivers, it is one of the few non-alcoholic cocktails that appears in classic cocktail books. The sharp tang of freshly squeezed fruit juices will make sure you keep a clear head.

INDEX OF FILMS AND FILM STARS

INDEX OF COCKTAILS

INDEX OF COCKTAILS BY INGREDIENT

CONTINUED

PICTURE CREDITS

• •

Film title: year of release; studio; stars; screenplay
MGM: Metro Goldwyn Mayer   TCF: Twentieth Century Fox
UA: United Artists

After Office Hours: 1935; MGM; starring Clark Gable and
Constance Bennett; screenplay by Herman J Mankiewicz.
All About Eve: 1950; TCF; starring Bette Davis and George
Sanders, Anne Baxter as Eve, and small part for Marilyn
Monroe; screenplay by Joseph L Mankiewicz; based on Mary
Orr's novel *The Wisdom of Eve.* **Angels Over Broadway:** 1940;
Columbia; starring Douglas Fairbanks, Jr and Rita Hayworth;
screenplay by Ben Hecht. **Anna Christie:** 1930; MGM;
starring Greta Garbo (in her first "talkie") and Charles Bickford;
screenplay by Frances Marion; based on play by Eugene
O'Neill. **Beloved Infidel:** 1959; TCF; starring Gregory Peck
and Deborah Kerr; screenplay by Sy Bartlett; based on book by
Sheilah Graham and Gerold Frank. **Blue Hawaii:** 1961; Hal B
Wallis/Paramount; starring Elvis Presley and Joan Blackman;
screenplay by Hal Kanter. **Breakfast at Tiffany's:** 1961;
Paramount; starring Audrey Hepburn and George Peppard;
screenplay by George Axelrod; based on novel by Truman
Capote. **Casablanca:** 1942; Warner; starring Humphrey
Bogart and Ingrid Bergman; screenplay by Julius J and Philip G
Epstein and Howard Koch; based on Murray Burnett's and Joan
Alison's play *Everybody Comes to Rick's.* **Cat on a Hot Tin
Roof:** 1958; MGM/Avon; starring Paul Newman, Burl Ives,
Elizabeth Taylor; screenplay by Richard Brooks and James Poe;
based on play by Tennessee Williams. **Circe, the Enchantress:**
1924; Tiffany Productions; starring Mae Murray and James
Kirkwood; Written by Vincente, Blasco Ibáñez. **DOA:** 1949;
UA/Leo C Popkin; starring Edmond O'Brien and Pamela
Britton; screenplay by Russel Rouse and Clarence Greene.
Dark Victory: 1939; Warner Bros; starring Bette Davis and
George Brent; screenplay by Casey Robinson; based on play
by George E Brewer and Bertram Bloch; Tallulah Bankhead
starred in the stage version; remade in 1963 and 1976.
Dead Reckoning: 1947; Columbia; starring Humphrey
Bogart and Lizabeth Scott; screenplay by Oliver H P Garrett
and Steve Fisher. **Dinner at Eight:** 1933; MGM; starring
John Barrymore and Marie Dressler, with appearance of
Jean Harlow; screenplay by Frances Marion and Herman J
Mankiewicz; based on play by George Kaufman and Edna
Ferber. **Don Juan Quilligan:** 1945; TCF; starring William
Bendix, Phil Silvers and Joan Blondell; screenplay by Arthur
Kober and Frank Gabrielson; from story by Herbert Clyde
Lewis. **Double Indemnity:** 1944; Paramount; starring Fred

MacMurray and Barbara Stanwyck; screenplay by Billy Wilder
and Raymond Chandler; based on a story by James Cain.
Every Day's a Holiday: 1937; Paramount; starring Mae West,
Edmund Lowe and Charles Butterworth; screenplay by Mae
West. **From Here to Eternity:** 1953; Columbia; starring Burt
Lancaster and Deborah Kerr, Frank Sinatra and Montgomery
Clift; screenplay by Daniel Taradash; based on novel by James
Jones. **Gone With the Wind:** 1939; MGM/Selznick; starring
Vivien Leigh and Clark Gable; screenplay by Sidney Howard
et al; based on novel by Margaret Mitchell. **Grand Hotel:**
1932; MGM; starring Greta Garbo; John Barrymore, Wallace
Beery, Lionel Barrymore, Joan Crawford; screenplay by William
A Drake; based on Vicki Baum's play by *Menschen Im Hotel.*
Guys and Dolls: 1955; MGM; starring Frank Sinatra, Marlon
Brando and Jean Simmons; screenplay by Joseph L
Manciewicz; based on play with book by Jo Swerling and Abe
Burrows; adapted from story by Damon Runyon. **How to
Marry a Millionaire:** 1953; TCF; starring Marilyn Monroe,
Lauren Bacall, Betty Grable and William Powell; screenplay by
Nunnally Johnson; based on play by Zoë Akins, Dale Eunson
and Katherine Albert. **Humoresque:** 1946; Warner Bros;
starring Joan Crawford and John Garfield; screenplay by
Clifford Odets and Zachary Gold; based on novel by Fannie
Hurst. **Island in the Sun:** 1957; TCF/Zanuck; starring James
Mason, Joan Fontaine and Harry Belafonte; screenplay by
Alfred Hayes; based on novel by Alec Waugh. **It Happened
One Night:** 1934; Columbia; starring Claudette Colbert and
Clark Gable; screenplay by Robert Riskin; based on Samuel
Hopkins Adam's story *Night Bus.* **Laura:** 1944; TCF; starring
Gene Tierney and Dana Andrews with Vincent Price and Clifton
Webb; screenplay by Jay Dratler, Samuel Hoffenstein and Betty
Reinhardt; based on novel by Vera Caspary. **Murder at the
Vanities:** 1934; Paramount; starring Kitty Carlisle, Jack Oakie,
Vincent McLaglen and Carl Brisson; screenplay by Carey
Wilson, Joseph Gollomb and Sam Hellman. **My Man
Godfrey:** 1957; Universal; starring David Niven and June
Allyson; screenplay by Everett Freeman, Peter Berneis and
William Bowers; Based on a screenplay by Morrie Ryskind and
Eric Hatch; based on Eric Hatch's novel *110 Park Avenue* .
Ninotchka: 1939; MGM; starring Greta Garbo, Melvyn
Douglas and Ina Claire; screenplay by Charles Brackett, Billy
Wilder and Walter Reisch; based on story by Melchior Lengyel.
Now, Voyager: 1942; Warner Bros; starring Bette Davis, Paul
Henreid and Claude Rains; screenplay by Casey Robinson;
based on novel by Olive Higgins Prouty. **Our Man in
Havana:** 1959; Columbia/Carol Reed (Kingsmead); starring
Alec Guinness, Noël Coward, Ralph Richardson, Maureen
O'Hara, Jo Morrow and Burl Ives; screenplay by Graham
Greene; based on novel by Graham Greene. **Our Modern**

Maidens: 1929; MGM; starring Joan Crawford, Douglas Fairbanks, Jr and Rod La Rocque; screenplay by Josephine Lovett. **Pal Joey:** 1957; Columbia/ Essex Sidney; starring Frank Sinatra, Rita Hayworth and Kim Novak; screenplay by Dorothy Kingsley; based on fictional letters by John O'Hara. **Paris in the Spring:** 1935; Paramount; starring Mary Ellis and Tullio Carminati; screenplay by Samuel Hoffenstein after play by Dwight Taylor. **Remember?:** 1939; MGM; starring Robert Taylor and Greer Garson; screenplay by Corey Ford and Norman Z McLeod. **Remember Last Night?:** 1935; Universal; starring Robert Young and Constance Cummings; screenplay by Harry Clork, Doris Malloy and Dan Totheroh; based on Adam Hobhouse's novel *Hangover Murders*. **Small Town Girl:** 1936; MGM; starring Janet Gaynor, Robert Taylor and James Stewart; screenplay by John Lee Mahin and Edith Fitzgerald; based on novel by Ben Ames Williams. **Sunset Boulevard:** 1950; Paramount; starring William Holden, Gloria Swanson and Eric von Stroheim; screenplay by Billy Wilder, Charles Brackett and D Marsham Jr. **Take One False Step:** 1939; Universal; starring William Powell and Shelley Winters; screenplay by Irwin Shaw and Chester Erskine; based on story by Irwin and David Shaw. **The Big Sleep:** 1946; Warner Bros; starring Humphrey Bogart and Lauren Bacall; screenplay by William Faulkner, Leigh Brackett and Jules Furthman; based on novel by Raymond Chandler. **The Girl Can't Help It:** 1956; TCF; starring Tom Ewell and Jayne Mansfield; screenplay by Frank Tashlin and Herbert Baker. **The Lost Weekend:** 1945; Paramount; starring Ray Milland and Jane Wyman; screenplay by Charles Brackett and Billy Wilder; based on novel by

Charles Jackson. **The Man Who Came to Dinner:** 1942; Warner Bros; starring Bette Davis and Monty Woolley, with Jimmy Durante making his screen debut; screenplay by Julius J and Philip G Epstein; based on play by George Kaufman and Moss Hart. **The Phantom Submarine:** 1941; Columbia; starring Anita Louise and Bruce Bennett; screenplay by Joseph Krumgold; based on story by Augustus Muir. **The Philadelphia Story:** 1940; MGM; starring Cary Grant (who donated his salary to war relief) Katherine Hepburn, and James Stewart; screenplay by Donald Ogden Stewart; based on play by Philip Barry. **The Roman Spring of Mrs Stone:** 1961; Seven Arts Productions; starring Warren Beatty and Vivien Leigh; screenplay by Gavin Lambert; based on novella by Tennessee Williams. **The Seven Year Itch:** 1955; TCF; starring Marilyn Monroe and Tom Ewell; screenplay by Billy Wilder and George Axelrod; based on play by George Axelrod. **The Snows of Kilimanjaro:** 1952; TCF; starring Gregory Peck and Susan Hayward; screenplay by Casey Robinson; based on story by Ernest Hemingway. **The Thin Man:** 1934; MGM; starring William Powell and Myrna Loy; screenplay by Frances Goodrich and Albert Hackett; based on novels by Dashiell Hammett. **To Have and Have Not:** 1945; Warner Bros; starring Humphrey Bogart and Lauren Bacall; screenplay by Jules Furthman and William Faulkner; based on novel by Ernest Hemingway. **Top Hat:** 1935; RKO; starring Fred Astaire and Ginger Rogers; screenplay by Dwight Taylor and Allan Scott; picture by RKO of the '30s. **Underworld:** 1927; Paramount; starring George Bancroft and Evelyn Brent; screenplay by Ben Hecht, Robert N Lee and Josef von Sternber.

Front cover: **Kobal Collection**/Metro-Goldwyn-Mayer. Back cover: **Kobal Collection**/Tiffany Productions
Aquarius Picture Library: Paramount Pictures Inc 34–35, 35; **The Ronald Grant Archive**: Columbia Pictures 90–91, 91, 92, 93, 96, 97; Metro-Goldwyn-Mayer 3, 22, 22–23, 70–71, 71, 78, 79, 100, 100–101, 104, 104–105; Paramount 9, 106, 107; Seven Arts Productions 84, 84–85; Twentieth Century-Fox 58, 59, 114–115, 115, 116, 117; United Artists Corporation 52, 53; Warner Bros; 94–95, 95; **Kobal Collection**: Columbia Pictures 42, 42–43, 50–51, 51, 62, 63, 64, 64–65; Metro-Goldwyn-Mayer 16, 17, 28, 28–29, 32, 33, 38–39, 46, 46–47, 60–61, 61, 72, 72–73; Paramount 10, 40, 40–41, 48, 48–49, 86, 87, 102, 102–103, 118, 118–119; RKO 76, 76–77; Tiffany Productions 110; Twentieth Century-Fox 13, 18–19, 19, 24, 25, 56, 56–57, 68, 68–69, 82–8; Universal 14, 20, 21, 112–113, 113; Warner Bros 26, 26–27, 30, 30–31, 44, 45, 54, 54–55, 66–67, 67, 74, 74–75, 98–99, 99; Warner Bros, Photo by Bert Six 88, 88–89

Acknowledgements

Many thanks go out to many who have offered advice and the occasional drink, but in particular a great debt of gratitude to Jane Clinton, whose assistance was invaluable; to Jake Arnott for his well-timed pick-me-up, and to Rosemary Markowsky for being the perfect chaser. Thank you also to the archives of the Ciné Club de Kennington and its curator Jon Davies; Simon and Martin at The Cinema Museum, Ronald Grant Archive; Dave Kent and Cheryl Thomas of the Kobal Collection; all at Compass and in California, Baltimore, New York and Hong Kong. Finally to our editors Jamie Ambrose and Hilary Lumsden for calling the shots; designers Gaye Allen and Colin Goody and all at Mitchell Beazley, with a very special thank you to Margaret Little for making it all happen. Cheers!